HEREFORDSHIRE

by

PADDY ARISS

Paddy Ariss

COUNTRYSIDE BOOKS

NEWBURY · BERKSHIRE

Cover illustration by Louis Mackay

Produced through MRM Associates Ltd., Reading
Typeset by Techniset Typesetters, Merseyside
Printed by Woolnough Bookbinding Ltd., Irthlingborough

CONTENTS

FOREWORD

There is no such thing as a typical privy. They come in all shapes and sizes, and may be built of wood, stone, brick or corrugated iron. They may stand under yew trees or right out in the open, or be so well concealed by shrubbery that they're hard to find. Some used to need emptying daily, others have never needed emptying at all. Every one is different.

The first person to whom I mentioned privies said, 'Oh, you won't find any of those around here nowadays!' I have been very happy to prove her wrong ... and I hope she reads this book. However, I was so worried she might be right that at first I photographed every collapsing shed that had ever held a seat and bucket, just in case nothing better turned up; after a while, I was getting quite choosy about ordinary single-seaters!

This project has been like a treasure hunt, with one clue leading to another, and getting more exciting all the time. For instance, the lady I first spoke to (and mentioned above) said, 'Always under yew trees, weren't they?' It took me a month to find out why.

My husband Peter comes from a long line of country carpenters, so no doubt his forebears would have built wooden privies and fashioned the seats for them. He also sold Bronco toilet rolls in the 1940s, at 19/11d for six dozen! My relations all had indoor loos, some with Bronco rolls, others with the traditional squares of newspaper. Many of their friends had privies, though, and I remember them clearly as a way of life in the 1930s and 40s, and in no way remarkable.

I do recall digging latrine ditches when I went camping with the Girl Guides. A canvas screen was the only shelter, and a shovelful of earth was sprinkled over the mess after each performance. Before we struck camp the ditch would be filled in, and we took pride in leaving no signs of our visit.

4

The only privy story in which I was personally (but thankfully only peripherally) involved occurred during a Youth Hostelling holiday in 1953. We were staying at a hostel where the privy was a dark and noisome hole in the ground; the bodily waste of dozens of squatting hostellers went straight into a gully leading to the river. Peter's sheathknife was a vital piece of equipment for cutting bread and opening tins – one morning while he was using the privy the precious knife slipped from its sheath and landed with a soft plop in the stinking mass below ... After spending some time trying to retrieve it without success, and ignoring the hostellers who were standing around having hysterics, he peeled off his shirt and plunged his arm down as far as he could. After an excruciating moment or two, he leaped to his feet with a yell of triumph and charged into the freezing river, repeatedly washing himself and his knife. Later that day, when he was slicing the bread for our lunch, our eyes met ... we both shrugged, and carried on. What else could we have done?

Forsan et haec olim meminisse juvabit. Perchance one day it will be a joy to remember even these things – my old school motto, and maybe that of all privy users of the past! They used to complain bitterly about having to trek down the garden in all weathers, dressing up in coats, scarves, gloves and boots on cold winter nights, sloshing through snow and mud and gales, enduring the scratchy paper, suffering the appalling smells at emptying time, and the flies, and the effort of digging holes for the waste ... yet nearly all the people I've interviewed appear to look back fondly on those days.

Very educational, privy-hunting: six months ago I knew practically nothing about them, now I'm giving talks on the subject! I recommend the pastime to anyone with an enquiring mind, a sense of adventure and, above all, a sense of humour.

PADDY ARISS

Privy-hunters venture forth in all weathers! I hadn't far to go for this one – almost opposite where I live in Eardisland. A modern seat on a very old hole.

[1]

Letting The Matter Drop

From mighty emperors to the poorest of peasants, we all have some things in common: we are born, and we will die. In between, we must eat and drink to live – and what goes in, must come out. And then we have to find somewhere to dispose of it.

No doubt, when Man first climbed down from the trees and walked upon two legs his sanitary arrangements were similar to those of the chimpanzee and the ape: if the results of their labours left them sticky and uncomfortable, they would have wiped their bums with leaves or grass, or rested their bottoms in a stream to wash away the mess.

> In days of old when knights were bold
> And lavatories weren't invented,
> They did their load in the middle of the road
> And went off quite contented.

As the 21st century dawns, it is important that privies are not forgotten; they are, after all, an important and necessary part of our social history. If their story is not told, and records made of the few still standing today, they may vanish into the mists of time.

So let me lead you down the garden path of history . . .

Many people are under the impression that nothing much happened between Day One and the 19th century, but archaeologists have unearthed proof of highly sophisticated sanitary systems dating back to the times of the ancient Greeks and Egyptians around 2,000 years BC, and later the Roman empire. The ancient Minoan palace at Knossos on the island of Crete is a prime example, with a system of sewers and latrines, washbasins and running water. They also had slaves to clean up where necessary; we have Harpic and Domestos!

We British are privileged to have the oldest known loo in the world, built 5,000 years ago in a stone house at Skara Brae in the Orkneys. However, right up until the Victorian sanitary inventions came along, posh plumbing was only for the privileged rich, the militia and the priesthood; the poor carried on as before.

The Romans built aqueducts, some of which are still standing, and they worshipped the goddess of sewers, Cloacina: around 520 BC they constructed the main channel of the sewage system in Rome, the Cloaca Maxima, the largest one of its kind at that date and still in use today. Large jars lined the streets for passers-by to pee in, but not everyone bothered to use them.

In 55 BC the Romans decided to pop over and conquer Britain, but they took one look at our lack of sanitation and went straight back home where things were far better arranged. In AD 43 they returned to these shores, possibly with a greater determination to show the natives the error of their ways.

The Roman militia stationed at Hadrian's Wall had 20-seater latrines, with sponge-tipped sticks for wiping their bums (they put the sponges back into a basin of water afterwards, for the next person to use; this was definitely a good reason for being first in the queue). I wonder whether they were ordered to report to do their duty in units of 20, at set times; or whether they were able to slope off for the Roman equivalent of a fag and a natter? At any rate, it was very much a social occasion.

With our traditional distrust of foreigners and their funny habits, the concept of hygiene never really caught on with the Brits, who heaved a collective sigh of relief and happily went back to their old ways when the Roman invaders finally departed after nearly 400 years.

For many centuries thereafter no significant technical developments came about in the history of plumbing, although one or two inventors had a go at improving the hygiene and coping with the problem of smells. Unfortunately, the Great British Public was still not interested, and it was not until the mid 19th century that people reluctantly started to take the matter seriously.

During the Middle Ages, military establishments catered for the needs of several hundred men in varying degrees of privacy and hygiene, and the nobility tried to introduce some sanitation into their castles. Situated on the Welsh borders, Herefordshire boasts a wealth of ancient castles, many originally built in Norman times and a few surviving today. Several have been altered and added to over the years, and some are still occupied. Garderobes were projecting overhangs, from whence the excrement of the occupants would fall to the ground or water below; mostly situated in a small chamber in an upper storey, within the thickness of the outer walls and at the end of a corridor to contain the noxious odours.

Rivers and streams were used for garderobes to empty into – Goodrich and Wilton castles are on the Wye; or a moat, as at Pembridge Castle where two closets overhung the water (in the far south of the county, nowhere near Pembridge village). The fish would feast off the excrement, and the castle's occupants would eat the fish . . . recycling is nothing new.

The lord of the castle would have had a seat to sit on, but lesser beings would just squat; the shit would fall just the same, straight down the outside of the wall, often leaving such a nasty brown sludgy stain that a stone corbel would eventually be built over it to conceal it.

The ruined red sandstone walls of Wilton Castle boast the

Well-maintained Goodrich Castle is one of the most complete mediaeval castles in the country, and includes the remains of six garderobes feeding one front tower, with collecting chambers and access from outside to facilitate cleaning. Note emptying hole below.

A stone corbel discreetly covers most of the staining from an early garderobe at Kentchurch Court, home of the Scudamores since 1086.

11

remains of at least two garderobes, one a multi-seater in the second storey room of a corner tower (now at ground level!), and the other a small single, set just within a doorway.

Wigmore Castle was the family seat of the Mortimers, in its day one of the most important border defences between England and Wales. The ruins have been made safe for the public to visit, and to my delight, I found the sites of several latrines and garderobes. One hole-in-the-floor 'long drop' has been covered with a stout iron grille to stop people falling down it.

A latrine opening can still be seen at Longtown Castle, but not only castles had them: Priscilla Flower-Smith has recently moved into a listed farmhouse near Longtown. 'There are fairly clear remains of a garderobe set against one wall,' she told me, 'and this was probably cleared out regularly by means of a stream which flowed nearby. The hole in the wall on the inside is now filled with a hot-water boiler (rather awkwardly). Architect's plans for the restoration/repair of the house have a loo in this spot, which seems fitting!'

Sanitary conditions in the bigger castles were really much better than one might think, most having privies in all the upper chambers. In some the privy would just be a hole to the side of the fireplace, and was often used as a 'priest's hole', where a hunted person could lie in hiding and hope to escape his enemies. King Henry III was very keen on good sanitation, and took a great interest in the facilities provided at the various castles he visited. He insisted that very deep pits were dug, and men were well paid to clean them out. The job of a gong fermor or farmer, so called because mediaeval privies were known as gongs, was for many centuries one of the best-paid jobs in the country.

It did occur to the wealthier people, towards the end of the Middle Ages, that something really ought to be done about the smells; and this led to the invention and use of portable close-

Herefordshire is renowned for its wealth of black-and-white houses. To find one with a garderobe was a real thrill! The picture shows a handsome Tudor garderobe to the left and above the porch at Upper Wythall, Walford, near Ross. The beautifully restored and carefully modernised 'loo with a view' is still in use.

stools, with lids that could be shut down to keep the odours from drifting out.

> There was an old man of Madrid
> Who went to an auction, and bid;
> The first thing they showed
> Was an ancient commode –
> My God, when they lifted the lid . . .!!

Monastery latrines were known as reredorters. The 'rere' bit was the same as 'rear'; it comes from Old French (sometimes we use their word *derrière* as another word for bum). Only the wealthy lords and ladies (who had servants to clean up after them) and the monks in the monasteries were interested in keeping themselves and their dwellings clean; but their fastidiousness paid off, as it helped many to survive the Black Death.

In the days when monasteries and abbeys were the centre of the local community, villagers would rely on the monks to provide them with vegetables and herbs for both cooking and for medicinal purposes. Flowers were grown only for decorating the churches, and for the houses of the wealthy – commoners had no use for them, and so had no need of gardens themselves. No gardens, no privies. They would have done their business on the fields or in the woods, wherever they happened to be when the need arose. Country people were advised to 'retire a bow's shot away' from the houses where they lived, and that advice, when it was taken at all, held good for centuries. Later, privies were built at a considerable distance from the house – a bow's shot? – to avoid polluting the well-water, and to keep the smells as far away as possible. However, when Henry VIII decided to put the kybosh on the abbeys and disperse the monks, the cottagers gradually began to grow their own plants by adapting the nearest bit of land, and cottage gardens came into being.

Tom Llewellin phoned me to say there was a 600-year-old *cistern* at Wigmore Abbey, and I got all excited; well, that's what I thought he said, but it must have been *system*. Just as interesting! Some pretty substantial ruins remain, and fortunately Henry left the 14th century Abbot's Lodging standing; it is occupied, and gradually being lovingly restored. I was shown the trapdoors in the floor of the Abbot's solar through which the contents of his lordship's bucket would be emptied into the water far below; water which had been diverted from the mill stream, and swept through below the house and then out to the marsh, along with all the detritus it collected en route. A very lush meadow has replaced the marsh. Surely this

The Abbot's Chair at Wigmore Abbey. The trapdoor leads to a water-filled culvert far below; the alcove (now housing a radiator) is where the Abbot sat to do his jobs!

was the 600-year-old *system*! The culvert tunnel is said to have connected with Paytoe Hall, where the nuns lived. (Nunnery loos were like the monastery ones: multi-holer reredorters.)

Outside, in a corner of the ruined abbey walls, stands a Victorian privy.

Many town and city dwellers used chamberpots and chucked the contents out of the bedroom windows. Sometimes they shouted 'gardyloo' (from the French '*gardez l'eau*'); mostly they didn't even bother to shout a warning, and indignant passers-by came in for a christening. My late father-in-law hated the entire French nation for the rest of his life after he suffered this indignity while marching through northern France during the 1914–18 war. It was probably he who taught my husband to sing:

15

Late 19th century privy, built into the ruined walls of Wigmore Abbey, lurks behind beams installed by English Heritage to support dangerous stonework. The author helps to prop up the beams . . .

> 'I passed by your window this morning at three,
> What was it, my darling, you emptied on me?
> I came back again at a quarter to four,
> Whoops! splash! you've done it once more!'

No wonder diseases were rife in olden times. The Middle Ages were so bad that they are sometimes referred to as the Midden Ages: the Romans had departed, and the inventive Victorians were yet to come.

Three of our kings were actually on the loo when they died, most embarrassing for the courtiers. I wonder how it was expressed in the Court Circular? Edmund Ironsides was stabbed in the back in 1016, murdered so that Canute could take over the throne;

16

George II was in his closet preparing himself for the arrival of his mistress when he suffered a massive stroke (too much excitement?); and James I of Scotland was murdered in an upstairs privy in 1437. Robert the Bruce, however, always carried his sword with him, even to the loo, and disposed of would-be assassins who attempted to catch him with his trousers down (or kilt up?).

Queen Elizabeth had one of the first royal flushes, invented and installed by her godson Sir John Harington. It was the first to have movable parts – a valve closet with a flushing cistern, cheap and practical, and one which used many devices similar to those we have today. He wrote an amusing book about it, giving full details to anyone wishing to build one, but apparently no one did, and the flush loo did not catch on for another 200 years. The book's title, shortened to *Ajax*, was a pun on 'jakes', another word for privy.

Leonardo da Vinci worked out a system of waste disposal for towns and cities, but in the 16th century people thought this just as crazy as his designs for submarines and helicopters.

Henry VIII liked to have his loo seat cushioned in velvet, trimmed with jewels and gold studs. Whenever the Court was in mourning (and with all those beheadings, that must have been quite often) black velvet was used.

I seem to remember a *Two Ronnies* TV show, when Ronnie Barker finished up with something like: 'We'll be taking a look at fur-covered toilet seats and asking: do they tickle your fancy?'

[2]

SOMETHING TO GO ON

A lavatory is for washing one's hands (I knew my school Latin lessons would come in handy some day; if I remember rightly, *lavabo* means 'I shall wash'). It was a Victorian euphemism which we still use to this day. 'I'm just going to wash my hands,' you say, and everybody knows perfectly well that what you mean is 'I'm going for a pee.'

Chambers Dictionary gives LOO as 'a lavatory. (Ety. dub.)'. The dubious etymology no doubt includes the derivations from gardyloo, bourdalou, and the Waterloo brand of cistern popular in Victorian times. It's a fairly modern word, so the latter sounds likely, but it's anybody's guess.

PRIVY is defined as 'a room set apart with container in which to evacuate body waste products, especially one in an outhouse.'

A place for *private* meditation, then. A place where one can be alone with one's thoughts. The present-day bathroom and loo still have that supreme advantage over other rooms in the house: one can retire and lock the door, leaving the screaming kids and the rest of the world outside. But somehow the modern style lacks the charm and the excitement of the earlier outside privies, which may date back to the early 17th century; there, unless one was caught short and had to do a lightning sprint to get there in time, one could wander down the garden path and sit in contemplation with a view through the half-open door and birdsong all around.

It was not always so.

Nowadays we tend to think of privies as being truly rural, mainly because most town and city ones were demolished long ago. In 1848, during the great cholera epidemic which

'I'm just going to powder my nose!' Sonia Taylor takes a look at the two-holer belonging to her neighbours Linda and Duncan Meakie at Welson, near Eardisley.

devastated Europe including Britain, the country dwellers got off lightly compared to the townsfolk, who lived in a state of unbelievable squalor.

People were only just beginning to understand that clean water supplies and proper sanitation would lead to better health for all, and that many diseases were preventable. Until this time, people relied on wells and public pumps for their water supply, or would draw it from adjacent brooks. Many wells were shallow, and contaminated by sewage seeping into them from cesspools. The first Public Health Act was passed in 1848, stating that no new houses could be built without having an earth or water closet. However, as its recommendations were not mandatory, authorities were slow to act upon them because they were unwilling to lay out the necessary cash.

Just off Kington High Street, these three privies served several cottages round a small courtyard. All are empty now, except for dead leaves; the hanging baskets make it a colourful corner in summer. Through the gate on the right, a neat brick path leads to the rear for emptying.

Later, councils had to spend several thousand pounds on sewers and waterworks. Deep wells were sunk and supplies of pure water were pumped through new pipelines to reservoirs on nearby hills; from there it flowed down to the towns.

By 1873, about half the townspeople had converted their privies and cesspits into water closets, which explains why so few privies are still to be found in urban areas – although a surprising number are still to be found in back gardens off Kings Acre Road, one of the main approaches to Hereford city from the west. Councils were reluctant to part with their money and sewage works were a long time coming, with the advent of the Second World War delaying their completion even further. In Leominster raw sewage was discharged into the river Arrow

A horse-drawn nightsoil cart at Yaidon Farm, Kington. Jonathan Mayglothling demonstrates the opening where bucket contents were thrown.

where it meets the Lugg. The smell was horrendous . . . Astonishing though it may seem, the first sewage disposal works did not come into operation there until 1963.

Officials used to test the water in wells from time to time – with a pocket microscope! When the cesspools were full, they were generally emptied after midnight, the 'nightsoil' being carried into the streets and removed in carts.

The horse-drawn muck carts of yesteryear were very different from today's modern waste disposal 'sludge-gulpers'. They would come around at night to empty the privies, and contents of the buckets would be tossed into a metal tank built into a cart with an opening lid. When the cart got back to the yard, a trap at the bottom of the tank would be opened in order to shed the load when the cart was tipped up (having first released the horse from between the shafts, of course!). Today's 'vintage' council lorries made their first appearance during the 1920s and 1930s, and the horses were retired.

Similar stories emerge from most of the towns in the county. Privy accommodation in Hereford, particularly amongst the poorer class of houses, was still very deficient in the mid 19th century. There was much overcrowding in the cottages, and in areas such as St Owen's Street there were 10 or 12 families using two privies.

Pigsties were very numerous in the heart of the city, as were abattoirs, each of the many butchers having his own. A law (which has not been repealed) stated that a man in charge of a horse and cart or cab must not leave them unattended; as a result, men were permitted to 'piss on the inside of the wheels' of their vehicles.

There used to be a 'house of office' on Wye Bridge in the 17th century; in the 19th there was still a gents' urinal there, and evidence of this survives in the fabric. There was another against the west wall of the tower of All Saints' church.

Wealthier residents with flush toilets could not obtain a suffi-cient volume of water to make them work properly, and in due course the waterworks tower on Broomy Hill was built to solve the problems; now a fascinating museum on the site tells the story and displays vast gas and steam engines used to pump clean river water from the Wye to city residents. The water-works itself is now powered by electricity. Even in the 1950s, however, loos in Hereford were very primitive for the times.

Cities and towns were obviously once very unpleasant places in which to live and work. After I'd read the fragrant details of the Public Enquiry held in Hereford in the middle of the 19th century, I found myself feeling heartily glad of our present boring, but effective, plumbing arrangements!

[3]

FLUSHED WITH SUCCESS

In 1775 Alexander Cummings came up with something so similar to the Elizabethan Ajax that one wonders whether he simply followed the instructions in Harington's book!

The local dialect expression 'Them be branners', meaning First Class, is probably a corruption of Bramah's – Joseph Bramah's water closet invention of the 1770s was supposed to be 'the best'. A century passed before anyone bettered it.

In the middle of the 19th century, the Rev Henry Moule designed a hygienic earth closet which successfully eliminated odours by covering the waste matter in the bucket with earth or ashes; by pulling up a handle set into the privy seat, a measured amount of earth was released from a hopper set on the wall behind the seat. When full, the bucket would be emptied onto the garden, where it mixed easily with the soil. Francis Kilvert, who was Vicar of Bredwardine and is buried there, says in his famous *Diary* that he met Moule and considered him a 'universal genius'. I found an earth closet in a barn at Stansbatch – the lid hinges were rusty but the handle still moved well enough. The closet was behind a partition in the far corner of the barn – no door!

The Big Three of early flush loos were George Jennings, Thomas Twyford and Thomas Crapper. Many people think that the word 'crap' originated with the latter, but in fact it is a fine old English word which has been in use since Tudor times. Thomas just had a name which was hilariously suitable for his job.

None of the three actually invented the flush toilet, but each designed improvements on earlier models; and the combination

MOULE'S EARTH CLOSETS

Apparatus on Bearers ready to Fix.
Deal Seat 3′ 0″ Long.

No. A1724. " Pull Out," as drawn.
No. A1725. " Pull Up " Pattern.
No. A1726. " Self-acting " Pattern.

Strong, Portable, Self-Contained Set. Plain Deal. Galvanized Fittings. Pail complete. 21″ Wide. 27″ Back to Front.

No. A1727. " Pull Out."
(as drawn)

No. A1728. " Pull Up "

Strong, Portable, Self-contained.
Best Plain Deal.
Fittings of Galvanized Iron.
With Pail complete.

No. A1729. Self-Acting. 21″ Wide.
27″ Back to Front. 36″ High.

No.		
A1724	..	.. 57/6
A1725	..	.. 70/-
A1726	..	.. 100/-
*A1727	..	.. 72/6
*A1728	..	.. 86/6
*A1729	..	.. 102/6

* Pails included.
Other Pails **3/7** Each Extra.

This ironmonger's catalogue of 1936 shows that the Rev Henry Moule's earth closets long continued to be popular.

This earth closet – with an odd seat on top of the hole – is at Stansbatch House, near Pembridge. The handle to release the earth or ashes is set behind the seat.

Thomas Crapper's Valveless Waste Preventer. (Photo by Simon Kirby)

of their efforts resulted in the modern flush, very much as it is today. Jennings designed a siphonic wash-down closet which increased the water pressure on entering the toilet bowl, so that the flush emptied and cleaned it better than on any previous model: Herefordshire has a fine working example at Eastnor Castle. Crapper designed the pull-chain with a valveless cistern high above the seat, decreasing the noise and conserving the water; and Twyford led the way in changing from cast-iron bowls to porcelain, which were much easier to clean and fun to decorate in glorious colours.

These inventions must have been good ones, as the royal family had the modern sanitary-ware installed at various palaces and stately homes. Several Jennings water closets were installed for the public at the Great Exhibition of 1851, and one penny was charged for using them – hence 'spending a penny'.

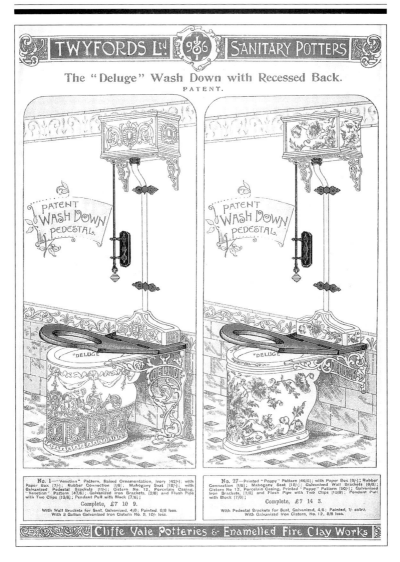

A page from an early Twyfords' catalogue. (Courtesy of Caradon Plumbing Solutions of Stoke-on-Trent)

Delightful Victorian loo, upstairs at Kentchurch Court.

The firm of Thomas Crapper & Co Ltd, which ceased trading in 1966, was revived in 1999 by businessman Simon Kirby, at premises in Warwickshire. 'For about £570 for a toilet named The Venerable, customers can recreate bygone bathroom elegance.' I felt that the location was out of bounds for a Herefordshire book until I discovered their retail outlet, The Bath & Beyond, is in Hereford itself! I promptly contacted Mr Kirby who was enormously helpful, sending me an excellent selection of photographs of Crapper memorabilia.

The firm of Thomas Twyford lives on, today incorporated in Caradon Plumbing Solutions of Stoke-on-Trent.

A Hereford company, Saunders Valves, was responsible for designing and perfecting a valve to operate a flush loo in aeroplanes flying at supersonic speed, in time for the Concorde to make use of it; impressed by this, the American Greyhound Bus Service installed it in its vehicles. Bob Morris worked for Saunders, and tested the valve for two years on his own loo at Shobdon (which had cesspit drainage in those days).

Bob's friend Bill Murphy has a 'green' privy in Shobdon, using rainwater to flush it. His kitchen extension houses a scullery, a privy and a coalhouse. Rainwater from the guttering collects in a tank set in the roof of the extension, and is used to flush the loo.

George Carter told me of 'a privy at Willey Chapel on the slopes of Stonewall Hill near Presteigne. This chapel (now a house) stood on the side of the hill miles from anywhere, lit by oil lamps – and yet it had a flush toilet! Rainwater collected on the roof was fed into a storage tank which supplied the toilet, which in turn emptied into a cesspit lower down the hill. Wonderful thing, gravity!'

[4]

PAPER AND PORCELAIN

From the dawn of history until comparatively recent times, people used to wipe their bottoms with their hands, or with grass, leaves, sticks and shells (the latter two must have been particularly uncomfortable). Going upmarket, the wealthy would sometimes use scraps of material to wipe their posteriors – pity the poor washerwomen! – and monks in the monasteries are said to have used pieces of their outworn robes.

It wasn't until the middle of the 19th century that paper became a commodity common enough to wipe bums with; *Old Moore's Almanac* became popular, and the tissue paper from around the oranges at Christmas (a seasonal treat, this). Eventually surplus paperwork was called bum fodder, later shortened to bumf and now known as junk mail!

Many families had a preference for which paper to use, the *Farmers Weekly* being the favourite in agricultural areas. The *Hereford Times*, of course, has wiped many a backside in this county, ever since its first issue in 1832. Old telephone directories were good too.

Nearly every woman I interviewed remembered the childhood task of cutting newspaper into squares, piercing a hole in one corner with a meat-skewer, and threading onto string or baler-twine for hanging on a nail in the privy. I even did it myself, for a thrifty aunt's indoor throne-room.

Public conveniences locally still tend to provide the hard, glazed Bronco-type of loo paper; apparently few people are so desperate that they want to pinch these rolls, whereas the soft toilet tissue disappears faster than it can be put out!

'Bromo' was one of the earliest commercial toilet papers to be

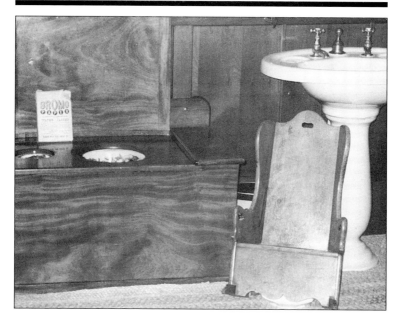

The beautifully preserved George Jennings flush loo at Eastnor Castle (circa 1870) and a child's rocking-chair with potty underneath. Superb mahogany everywhere in this Victorian bathroom.

sold, in a flat pack of separate sheets. It is still to be found in Eastnor Castle beside a magnificent George Jennings flush loo (but not for use: a roll of the soft stuff is provided). Perforated sheets didn't make their appearance until the 1880s.

Do you know that toilet rolls caused 24 serious accidents in the UK in 1994? Don't ask me <u>how</u>!

In Georgian times, it was quite common for the gentry to go on a pot behind a pillar, or even in front of one, in full view of other guests enjoying their dinner. A servant would empty the pot, of

31

Jane Jenkins of Holmer WI with her Aunty's commode. Aunty used it to hide her savings – never for the purpose intended!

With TV antiques expert Henry Sandon and some of his porcelain potties, in Hereford, September 1999. The tall pot is from the New Forest area, circa 1600; the sauceboat-shaped bourdalou was used by ladies, modestly concealed beneath their voluminous skirts.

course. Guests would even be received by their host when he was enthroned, perhaps on a close-stool (forerunner of the commode, defined by *Chambers Dictionary* as 'a night-stool', and said to have been invented by the Roman Commodus in the 2nd century AD).

Having a chamberpot under the bed saved one from a trip down the garden in the dark. Nowadays potties are more often used for toddlers and invalids, and the seriously sick are subjected to hospital bedpans. Most of the beautifully decorated Victorian gazunders are now either museum pieces or used to hold plants. Early potties were of plain earthenware, but when porcelain became popular they were often colourfully decorated. I came across one with a picture of a frog inside and the verse:

'Keep me clean and use me well,
And what I see I will not tell.'

A huge Tudor tome in the Record Office, *Ancient Customs of the City of Hereford*, states that no one was allowed to empty their chamberpots into the streets (a nasty habit which existed amongst townspeople from Roman times until the early 20th century). Regardless of the Law, people continued doing it. Again, the wealthy people would have had no need to – their servants dealt with such things.

Priscilla Davies of Weobley remembers that a 'lady' known as Sixpence (the rate she charged?) lived in Hay-on-Wye; the wife of one of her gentleman friends decided to get her revenge by emptying the contents of her po onto Sixpence when she passed below, shouting 'You had him last night, now you can have his remains!'

Sophia Loren, in her cookery book of favourite recipes, wrote, 'Eels have become one of my favourite meals after a tremendous experience I had with them on the Po.'

[5]

AT YOUR OWN CONVENIENCE

Herefordshire is a largely agricultural county with just one smallish city, five market towns, and innumerable villages and hamlets – ideal hunting grounds for research into privies.

Allan Lloyd, a well-known resident of Kington near the Welsh border, gave me the following advice on how and where to build a privy, based on his own personal experiences:

'The privy/necessary house/*ty bach* [Welsh for small house] should be placed discreetly at the bottom of the garden and obscured from view by a hawthorn or holly tree planted specifically at the rear of the privy; this is also a preventive measure to avoid would-be passers-by from causing a nuisance by knocking or throwing stones at the back timbered/galvanised wall of the occupied building.

'It should be positioned in line with the front of the cottage or dwelling, so that light from the windows can guide one's return during the hours of darkness.

'A log pile should be placed conveniently at the side of the privy to make the necessary journey even more productive and purposeful; it is also useful to disguise one's intention when approaching or leaving the area of the privy at a time when a "respectable" visitor such as the vicar makes an unexpected call – abort the operation if necessary by collecting an armful of firewood and thus avoid any embarrassment to either party.

'Where possible, the unit should be placed over a stream – it is much more hygienic (though perhaps not for those living further downstream and relying on the water for their drinking supplies).

'The *ty bach* should be built to precise measurements. For

A single-seater beside a stream – Betty Lane of Dorstone tries this one for size . . .

instance, the seat should be of sufficient height for the sitter to avoid being splashed when deposits hit the stream below, and sufficiently high to avoid the occupant being singed by paper boats passing below, having been set alight by knowledgeable lads!

'The door should always be hung to open inwards, making locks or bolts unnecessary so long as the distance between seat and door makes it possible to extend the legs from a seated position, to be braced against the door. The obligatory motif carved into the door is not for decoration purposes, but to observe any movement towards the privy; or to enable the sitter to remain in occupation until a caller has moved out of view.

'Placed within easy reach should be a bundle of local newspaper squares, torn purposely to size and held together with binder twine on a side wall hook. Pieces of such newspaper will in this way provide a useful and profitable opportunity to keep up with the local news.

'Be careful in your choice of wood for the seat, so as to avoid splinters.

'Communal privies with holes of varying sizes will be necessary if there are children living at home – particularly as they always seem to have a great urgency of requirement.'

Which reminds me of the advice from Andrew Boorde (1500–1549):

'Beware of draughty privys and of pyssinge in draughts,
and permyt no common pyssinge place about the house
– and let the common house of easement to be over
some water or else elongated from the house.
Beware of emptynge pysse pottes and pyssing in chymnes.'

Of course, not everyone was fortunate enough to have a stream

This family three-holer stands under a yew tree, well away from the house at Burlton Court, Burghill.

A small piece is missing from the child's seat.

handy, eliminating the necessity of emptying yucky buckets – owners could opt for any of four main types; cesspit, bucket, earth closet or water closet.

Pits were the best bet where big families were involved, as they seldom needed emptying, if ever. The privy would be built over a large deep pit lined with brick or stone; bodily waste would drop through from the seat above, liquids leaching away into surrounding soil. Some pits were limed, others just let nature take its course, and in due time the almost odourless, friable material could be dug out and used to add excellent nutrients to the vegetable garden. When emptying was needed, either the council muck-cart, or Dad, would oblige – this is when long-handled scoops came in useful.

Buckets were the most widely used receptacle, mostly under a hole in a wooden box seat. Some would have a door at the front of the seat for removal of the bucket when it needed emptying, others had a hinged seat which was raised to take out the bucket. Many had a hole at the rear of the building for this purpose. Embarrassed sitters caught unawares have been known to clench their sphincter muscles while the bucket was being emptied behind them ... the disposal of the contents is vividly described by those whose memories I have recorded, although in some areas the council cart would pay a weekly visit.

The simplest earth closet was where a bucket of earth or ashes would be provided for the privy user to scatter a handful over his or her offerings, thus helping to eliminate smells and discourage flies. Posher types included those with a handle to release earth from a hopper, like the one that the Rev Henry Moule invented.

Some enterprising WC owners have converted their privies into 'modern' flush loos by connecting a cistern; before use, the cistern has to be filled from a conveniently-placed water-butt! I have also seen several outside flush loos, very useful when gardening and not wanting to drag muddy boots into the house.

Back-to-back one-holers share a stone building with back-to-back pigscots, under a yew tree and a long way from the house at Lower Hengoed.

The Hereford Records office holds details and costs of building Retch Cottage in 1832. It is interesting that 'labor' is spelled the American way; and the total cost was £97.12s.7d. The privy there was not erected until three years later! It cost 17s.4d: carpenter's wages 13s.1d, timber 4s.3d.

During my researches, I wondered why privies were often under yew trees; the most likely explanation is that flies and bluebottles dislike the smell of yew, so privies were sited beneath the trees to keep the insect pests at a distance. It was believed that the guardian spirit of the house lived in the yew tree.

Privies often seem to have been located beside pigsties (or pigscots, as they are known locally); the smells must have blended nicely. There is an excellent example at Lower Hengoed, on the Welsh border. I got well and truly lost when I

18th century privy at Hollytree Cottage, Goodrich, family home of Roland Trafford-Roberts (pictured). Two side-by-side singles with pigsties behind.

went to visit it, along a maze of unsignposted lanes, but it was worth it. A tiny stone barn was situated a long way from the house, near the fence into a field. The barn was neatly divided down the middle, lengthwise – the house had once been two cottages. Two thirds of each section had once housed pigs; just beyond this, a low wall stretched a few feet on either side, giving some privacy from the pigs to those using the single-seater privy beyond. Or maybe to give the pigs privacy from the sitters! The privies were back-to-back.

Norman Smith used to live in Bartestree as a boy, and the privy was a long way down the garden. He used to fetch his bike out of the coal shed by the house and ride it down to the privy, which was a family three-holer with one small and two big holes, and wooden lids. Adjacent to the pigsties, it was a back-to-back earth closet which his father used to empty with an old saucepan! He grew very fine vegetables – cucumbers and tomatoes used to grow where none had been sown . . .

When the boy went to visit his grandmother at Ashperton, he had to go through the chicken pen to reach the privy – and had to run the gauntlet of hens pecking at his legs! Only the Ledbury newspapers were used for the privy there.

Old Ebeneezer's young nephew was up from London, and needed to use the toilet. He was shown the way, down the garden path, past the pigscots. He returned almost at once, saying he couldn't possibly go where there were so many flies about. Ebeneezer consulted his turnip watch. 'Ar,' he said, 'if you can just wait five minutes, the missus'll have the joint on the table by then, and all the flies will go there.'

[6]

PRIVY-HUNTING

Joan Hutchinson sent me a map reference for finding a privy in Colva parish, in use until 1993; first, I had to learn how to interpret a map reference! Hunting privies has turned out to be a real education, in so many ways.

In 1953 the 17th century Trafford Almshouses in Pembridge were described as having 'a door at the back of the living-room which leads out to the back gardens, where there is a Ladies at one corner and a Gents at the other. The occupants of the six houses have to carry their water from the nearest village pump.'

It was not until 1967 that indoor loos were installed, and one of the privies was demolished. The other, minus its seat, was left standing by the Trustees 'as a reminder of the past, but mainly to support the ivy covering the roof!' This was the first privy I photographed; I had lived next door for 22 years and never noticed it . . .

Daphne Fannin showed me a spring in her garden at Titley where the first privy had been, and then, near a pool, the sad remains of two side-by-side ones which had been in use when the house was two cottages. They had been ivy-covered, but the privies collapsed when the ivy died! A modern privy with an Elsan at the side of the house was the only convenience available when the owners moved in during the 70s.

There is a privy situated on the banks of a stream at a farm well off the beaten track, not far from Pudleston. I had to drive along the sort of lanes which have grass growing in the middle, and where you pray that you don't meet anything coming the other way. The privy is in good condition and has two holes, one slightly smaller than the other; Edward Bostock, the young

Jean Richards battles her way through the nettles to reach an old three-holer, still intact, at Walford, near Brampton Bryan.

44

Two-holer (still usable) over the Whyle Brook near Pudleston. It never needs cleaning out.

man who showed me round, could remember using it as recently as the 1980s when a septic tank had been installed. The privy is stone built, and has a small window, but no door. Through the holes I could see the gleam of water from the Whyle Brook six feet below. The privy never needs clearing as the water washes everything away very satisfactorily.

I have recently learned that a running stream will break up faeces before it has travelled a dozen feet. I now feel better about all the poor souls living downstream of others.

The Garnons at Byford is one of Herefordshire's stately homes where a wooden privy for the use of the estate workers is still standing. Sir John Cotterell, whose family have lived here for generations, took me up the hillside at the rear of the home farm – someone had very kindly chopped back the bracken and brambles; it was about as far from the farm as it could be! The privy is a single-seater, with the bucket still in place although it had crumbled to half its original size. There would have been about twenty workers when it was last used.

Near Dilwyn, there's an unusual assortment of privies at the Hall family's Bidney Farm. When the farmhouse was two cottages a long brick wall divided them at the back, with a single privy on one side and two on the other. They are of the same mellow brick as the high wall itself, and have corrugated iron roofs. For once, no attempt at concealment with trees or bushes has been made. On the other side of the wall from the single, attached to a small farm building and quite near the house, is an intriguing arrangement of two very different singles under the same roof, entered through one open doorway. One is a one-holer bucket-type loo, emptied from the rear, and the other is an earth closet with a cupboard-like ash container behind the seat. The interiors to all loos were plastered.

Mr and Mrs Lloyd of Menalls Farm at Kimbolton very kindly cleared all the garden stuff out of their privy (always a good place to store pea-sticks!) to reveal a fine brick-built two-seater, with the holes quite close together. Covered with a thick roof of ivy, it is a lean-to against a high brick wall. Back-to-back, in the field beyond a wire fence, stands the roofless and empty remains of another brick privy, originally for the use of the farm workers; now occasionally used by the horse, who obviously thinks it's like the stall in his stable. The rear disposal holes for the two-seater are clearly visible from the field.

Many old privies now house garden tools and all sorts of odds and ends; some are woodsheds or henhouses, some still retain the seat, and others are even usable if not actually in use – I found only one still in constant use, at The Clouds near Checkley, but I know of others. The Checkley privy needs emptying only once in every 3 or 4 years – not an unpleasant job as the material is

Mrs Lloyd helps to clear all the garden stuff out of the two-holer at Kimbolton for me to photograph. Pea-sticks much in evidence! Note how the privy is on the far side of the wall from the house. Nice view.

friable, not smelly, and goes on the compost heap. A modern seat over an ancient hole, a piece of greenery, soft toilet paper and even a mirror make it an agreeable garden retreat.

A large stone-built three-holer at Stocktonbury has been transformed into an elegant summerhouse, with white panelled interior walls decorated with paintings of flowers; a horseshoe-shaped seat, and a sundial in front among the roses complete the picture. Owner Mary Treasure very kindly sent me photographs, and her husband Raymond told me on the phone that there used to be three equally large privies in a row, but the other two (of brick) were for the servants and were knocked down some time ago. The servants' privies adjoined the posh one, separated only by a wire fence; the disposal boxes for all three were chained together, so that they could be pulled out

This privy at The Clouds, near Checkley, is still in constant use, an agreeable garden retreat. A sculptured head on the outside wall is of Silvanus, Roman god of the countryside and gardens – I was hoping it might have been one of the sewer gods, Crepitus or Stercutius!

48

Roosting boxes built above the three-holer privy seat at Whitecross Farm, Bridstow. The hen was camera-shy!

The old three-holer at Stocktonbury is now an elegant and charming summerhouse. (Photo by Mary Treasure)

from one end to empty. Young Raymond used to get into trouble playing trains with them!

Another new use for an old privy is to be found at Whitecross, Bridstow, the family farm of Angie and Tim Hoddell. The house was built in 1875, and presumably the privy was built about the same time. It's a three-holer of red brick, with a corrugated iron roof replacing earlier pantiles. Tim can remember playing in the privy as a boy. Until recently it had been used to store the mower and roller for the tennis court, but when Angie acquired some chickens she decided to give them an elegant home. Roosting boxes were built directly above the bench seat with its three holes, and the hens settled in happily.

Not all my clues in the hunt led to treasures. Alec Haines phoned to say he'd found the iron seat of a two-holer in his shed; my husband took the call while I was out. An *iron* seat? It certainly sounded unusual, if not comfortable. I rang Alec. By this time, 'the sons' had had a look at it – and had decided that it was the top of an old Rayburn stove, very similar in size and shape to a privy seat. Ah well, you can't win 'em all.

[7]

PANIC IN THE PRIVY

Rats were often quite a problem. Kath McGowan of Pembridge was always afraid that one would pop up from the murky depths and bite her bare bum! and another friend always used to take her Jack Russell terrier with her to chase the rats away when she visited the privy. When George and Mary Carter first moved into Kimbolton Court, there were no mod cons and the privy had to be used. George describes the facility as 'like the house, stone built, but thatched with tin. It was a friendly little place, being a two-seater where we could sit side by side holding hands. The procedure for entering this delightful little grotto was to kick the door hard, then wait for the rats to disperse!'

Several people had a terror of nameless horrors lurking in the pit below ... with good reason, as this account from Mrs Sylvia Griffiths of Clehonger will show:

'Throughout most of my childhood I lived in Wormsley, an isolated hamlet near Weobley; we had the usual outside toilet about fifty yards from the house.

'One evening in 1937, when I was 10 years old, we heard my Dad calling from the back door. Mum and I answered his call, only to find him holding tightly to the seat of his trousers. My mother released his trousers and as they fell to the floor, so did a large dead rat. Luckily Dad's tight grip had killed it.

'Of course there was no means of lighting in the toilet so he was unable to see what he described as a "pawing around his shoes". Thinking it was our cat, he took no notice – until it ran up his trouser leg.'

Margaret Thomas of Pembridge told me about the trouble which befell her cousin's little boy. He had been using the two-

This two-holer at Kingsthorne was in use until 1990. Is that a bucket in front of the privy? (Photo courtesy of Sally Dymott)

holer, which was one of those with round lids which fitted neatly into the holes: unfortunately, he put the small lid onto the big hole, and it vanished into the murky depths. Knowing that he would be unpopular to say the least, he went in after it ... He succeeded, but had to be scrubbed down with bucketfuls of water and a broom before being allowed into the house! Margaret remembers that lime was used on her own family privy, which was always called the dub.

Another Pembridge lady recalls that her grandmother went out to the privy late one night, and got a helluva shock when she found it already occupied! An old tramp was sound asleep in there, snug and dry. This was not uncommon in those days.

Ron Jones of Pembridge remembers Stingo Bill, who was a nice enough fellow, but he did tend to drink too much in the

This privy at Wellbrook, Peterchurch, was certainly some distance from the house. In use during the 1950s and still usable today, it's a single, stone-built in the 19th century. No attempt at concealment for a change!

village pubs. One time they found him on his hands and knees, trying to roll up the white line down the middle of the road thinking it was a bandage. Some nights it would be gone midnight before he got home, but it was his habit to retire to the privy last thing before he went to bed, and there he would sing at the top of his voice. He had a good voice, but it was **loud**; he could be heard the other end of the village. Mostly he used to sing 'Galway Bay', and the neighbours used to holler at him to belt up. One night Stingo's brother Bob could stand it no longer, and went round to the back of the privy with a pile of old newspaper. He took down the cover and shoved the paper into the hole which was used for emptying, then set light to it . . . Stingo leapt up with a yell and went charging down the path to his cottage, his trousers at half-mast. The singing stopped. A photo of

Stingo Bill can still be seen in the New Inn (which has been 'new' for several centuries).

An anonymous informant telephoned me with this story, which he swears is true. 'My aunt always used to tell me this bit of family history, about my grandfather who was employed as a gardener by the Barneby family in the old estate gardens at Bredenbury Court and Longworth Hall.

'A rather small and very gloomy privy was provided in the gardens for the use of the estate workers. One day when my grandfather was working in the kitchen garden, he felt the need to go, so he retired to the privy, pulled his trousers down, and sat on the seat. In the meanwhile, a maid had come into the garden to collect herbs and vegetables, and thought she might as well pay a visit while she was at it. She went to the privy. Upon entering, and not noticing Grandfather on the seat in the gloom, she pulled her knickers down – and sat down on his lap.

'On feeling bare legs beneath her, she leapt up with a shriek, adjusted her dress, and very quickly left the kitchen garden.'

Mary Needham of Lyonshall told me about a friend of hers, the mother of a large family, who had an unforgettable experience one hot summer afternoon when she paid a visit to the privy at the far end of the garden. Most people in those days kept a few chickens and a pig or two, and this family was no exception. Earlier in the day, the old sow had happened on a wheelbarrow full of rotting fallers from the perry-pear tree, and had enjoyed an unaccustomed feast. By the time Mother went to the privy, with her mind on other things, the sow was rolling drunk; it staggered all over the orchard and finally collapsed in a heap against the privy door.

As the door opened outwards, the lady was penned inside; she wondered what on earth had occurred when she heard the great thud, followed by loud snoring and hiccuping. Well, she pushed and pushed on that door, but the old sow weighed a ton and she

Servants' privy (back-to-back with the gardeners') at the Old Vicarage, Titley. The interiors of both are collapsing into the stream below – a little bridge arch can be seen to the right.

couldn't shift her. As she was often to say later, 'Have **you** ever tried shifting a drunken sow?' And there Mother sat, the whole afternoon, until somebody heard her yells for help and came to free her. That was a very long and uncomfortable afternoon, she said. Privies are not built for comfort, and the day was hot, the flies were busy, and the smells were not so good either.

[8]

POSH PRIVIES

A fine Georgian house at Luntley, near Pembridge, has a privy with a difference. When Roger and Margaret West moved in, in the sixties, there were no mod cons and the outside privy had to be used. It was such a delightful two-holer that they made a feature of it, with a patio in front. Wooden garden seats and a table stand in front of the white-painted door, and Virginia creeper covers the little building which has a much larger window than is usual in privies. The huge pit below never needed emptying or cleaning, and smells were never a problem. One of the seats is a child's, lower than the other; Mother-in-law used to complain that one was too high and the other too low!

Margaret used to call big jobs 'shunting trucks'; her mother would ask her, 'Have you shunted your trucks today?' Roger told me of a father's advice to his son: 'Keep your feet warm, your head cool, your bowels open and your mouth shut.'

The Staick House in Eardisland dates back to the 14th century, and still retains many of its original features. It is black and white, and the privy matches the house: oak beams and whitewashed plaster, a window with leaded lights, and tiled roof. Pat Roche and I had to fight our way through a jungle to reach it, under the gloomy shade of several gigantic yew trees. It is a two-holer, but definitely not in use as there were several old car seats piled up on top; it must have had a deep cesspit as there were no visible means of emptying. It is a very large and spacious privy, as befits the big house, with plenty of room between the two holes.

Robert Devereux of Brook House, Mathon, has a wonderful two-holer. The holes are 7″ (for a child) and 9.5″ in diameter,

The Luntley two-holer (note large window) has become a feature of the lovely garden. It was in use until the mid 1960s.

The early 17th century two-holer beside the Cradley Brook at Mathon. All the boards are pegged, not nailed. (Photos courtesy of Ted Stewart and Robert Devereux)

cut out of two planks, with walls five foot high and the same in width; these are not wattle and daub, but simply boards attached to beams, and pegged (not nailed) throughout, except for the door which is of later, ordinary design. The privy has a simple roof of red tiles, the floor is of loose bricks, and it is very likely that there used to be a gully going directly into the Cradley Brook, only a few feet away. The privy may be the same age as the house, which is early 17th century.

I visited a retired doctor who owns a delightful three-holer at Burlton Court, Burghill. Well away from the handsome house and many outbuildings, the brick-built privy sits alone under yew trees. Dr McGlashon had thoughtfully placed a ladder at the small window so that I could get a good angle for my photograph; when I found it was too dark inside to focus properly, he fetched a strong lamp and a very long extension lead – as a photographer himself, he not only understood my problems but had the wherewithal to solve them. The loo itself was enchanting, with a very tiny seat set at an angle just below and in front of the adult bench seat.

Oddly enough, Marion Rees of Haymeadow Farm at Burghill has a three-seater of almost identical design at the bottom of her garden – only the lids were different. As it is just across the fields from Burlton Court, my guess is that it may well have been built by the same person. It was in use until 1954 when an upstairs loo was installed; the 'garden room' was then used only in an emergency, and by Marion's grandchildren who prefer the novelty, picking raspberries and strawberries as they go down the long pathway.

A few miles up the road, in Tillington, Marion's sister Mrs Norah Palmer told me that they always had to use the hurricane lamp to go down the garden to the lav at nights. 'Granny Thomas and other relations used to save their newspapers for us. Dad used to use an old tin wheelbarrow to empty out the

Marion Rees and friend outside the privy at Haymeadow Farm, Burghill.

Entrance to the three-holer at Haymeadow Farm, showing roof detail. (Photo by Marion Rees)

muck in a field. We always called it the lav, or just going down the garden. "Pee for a penny, a halfpenny won't do," we used to say.' Mrs Palmer lived at the farm until quite recently, using the privy as there were no mod cons; she now lives with a daughter who has an indoor loo. Her granddaughter Joanna lives at the old farm, where she and her husband are gradually updating the home comforts. However, the two-holer is still in the garden – with an old Elsan perched on top of the seat!

There is a very grand listed privy near Ross-on-Wye. It is 18th century with later alterations, and is built of sandstone and brick with a Welsh slate roof. Rectangular in shape, it has a brick entrance arch, a small outlet chute at the back, and a battlemented parapet; and not only does it have a two-seater earth closet inside, it also boasts a waiting room! Sadly, I was not able to photograph this treasure.

Mrs Legge of Pencombe sent me a fine photograph of the family three-holer. She wrote, 'My father-in-law built this privy in the early 30s at Shortwood, Pencombe, after the small one they had before had been blown down. The seat was roughly sawn out of a tree off the farm by himself and a workman – they also erected the building of stone and concrete. As they were a very large family (17 children) he decided on the three-holer, and it was used until the 1960s as the only toilet, and is still usable now (though a bit rough!). In the War we had evacuees from London who continued visiting after the war; the long walk down the garden was a great joke to them, especially the privy.'

Shortwood, still a working farm, is now open to the public, and children are able to see how cows are milked, play with the small animals – and giggle over the contrast between the little privy and their own modern loos. The farm is set on a hill, with wonderful views over Herefordshire.

Great Parton Farm is a gracious Jacobean house of blackened beams and mellow brick, near Eardisley. The privy, modestly

Three-holer built by John Legge at Shortwood, Pencombe, in the early 1930s, for his family of 17 children! It was in use until the 1960s, and is still usable. (Photo courtesy of Mrs I. K. Legge)

The shaded entrance to the superb three-holer at Great Parton Farm, near Eardisley.

Interior of the three-holer at Great Parton Farm. The author takes a pew!

screened by shrubbery and covered with ivy, is a magnificent three-holer in excellent condition. It has a flagstone floor, a small window on each side of the building, and a very good door with an iron latch. The three holes are of varying sizes, with the child's seat much lower than the other two. This is another loo with a pit below, which has never needed emptying.

It's the only privy I have found which is reputed to have had a distinguished posterior parked upon it: Mrs Churchill's during one of her visits to Herefordshire. Winston Churchill held secret wartime conferences at Dunfield House, a secluded mansion on the Welsh border near Kington, so it may well be true.

Roger West told me the story of how the Lord Privy Seal was extremely rude to Churchill in the House one day, the latter being in Opposition at the time. The Leader of the House told him to apologise to Churchill, so off he went to the great man's house and rang the doorbell. The butler answered, and took a message to his master, who was in the loo. He knocked on the door and said, 'The Lord Privy Seal is here to see you, sir.' Churchill replied, 'Tell the Lord Privy Seal that I am sealed to my privy, and can only deal with one shit at a time.'

I think the really Perfect Privy must be the three-seater in the Avoncroft Museum of Historic Buildings near Bromsgrove, Worcestershire. It went there from Leominster in 1984, when Hereford and Worcester were one county (now separated again, after an amicable divorce in the late 90s). The building is approximately 12′ square, and is a charming and rare survival, the sort of 'temple of convenience' that wealthier folk were wont to build, unlike the crude erections of the less well-to-do.

This fascinating privy was originally built in the grounds of

Townsend House, a Leominster mansion in Green Lane, during the first half of the 18th century. The three holes (2 adult and 1 child) are set into a box bench, and would have been sited over a deep cesspit. The Museum was told about the privy by the conservation officers of Leominster District Council in 1981; the building was later dismantled and re-erected at the Museum. It was opened to the public by Mollie Harris in 1984; Mollie, of course, having become famous for her own books about privies, as well as for her role as Martha in *The Archers*.

A Stoke Prior WI member told me that the 'Leominster Loo' was once used by a well-known visitor, a singer who had come to give a concert in the house next door. Asking for a quiet place where she could practise her singing before the evening's performance, she was shown to the privy at Townsend House. She was startled to be told that it had 'the best acoustics in town' – and so it proved.

My most exciting find was another very superior Leominster privy, situated just outside the town at Dishley Court, where the old barns have been converted into Tudor-style houses. Quite close to the original farmhouse, partially screened by small trees and on the edge of a small stream, is a magnificent FIVE-holer! The building is roughly 7' × 5', made of mellow brick with peg tiles on a single pitch roof and a plastered interior. Parallel with the stream and running the length of the building is a bench seat with two widely-spaced holes, obviously made for adults with amply-proportioned buttocks; at right angles to the main bench is a much lower one, with two tiny holes, all four holes varying in size. The big mystery, however, is the fifth hole, which is about the size and shape of an A4 sheet of paper, and is situated centrally between the two adult holes. All the holes have lids, but this rectangular one has a knob handle with

Taken through the window! The FIVE-holer at Dishley Court (the fifth hole is bottom right, in front of those pictured). The stream can be seen below if one looks down through the holes.

which to lift it. So what was the purpose of this hole? Not to hold paper, for all holes lead directly to the stream, which can be seen below; nor to empty potties, for the adult holes were quite big enough for that. Someone suggested it could be for a man to use (standing) if all the seats were occupied!

[9]

PLEASE MISS, MAY I BE EXCUSED?

Janet Morgan is the Secretary at Kingsland Primary School. She went to school in Eardisland, where the boys' privies were back-to-back with the girls'. There were only three cubicles, with bucket-type loos, and the children used to play 'eeny, meeny, miny, mo' to see who would be first to use them; often some poor child would wet her pants if she lost.

Many school privies remain in use in Herefordshire, although they are now flush toilets; but the children still have to cross the playground to reach them. Dilwyn is one of these, and Kingsland's outside loos were rebuilt.

Allan Lloyd told me that primary schools always had multiple 'opportunities'. At Lady Hawkins School in Kington where he taught for 40 years, it is on record that in 1892, after bestowing considerable praise on the Headmaster for his work, the governors, in case the Master should become complacent as a result of such praise and attention, reminded him of his 'other important responsibilities, namely that he would be requested from time to time to see that the closets and urinals are kept clean and in good order.' Some 18 months later Headmaster Thomas Henry Williams resigned; no reason for his decision is recorded.

The playground at the little school in Kilpeck was divided down the middle: boys to one side, girls to the other. At the bottom of the playground area were the privies, where the boys would run along the back pushing nettles through the bucket openings in the hope of stinging the little girls' bare backsides!

A telephone caller told me that his school had a separate privy for the teachers; if the teacher was unpopular, the boys would lie in wait to apply the nettles, then run like hell.

Interesting rear view of a Mathon single-seater, showing unusual window and clearly-defined emptying hole (ideal for nettles). It has a red tiled floor, and the seat has a full-length lid. (Photo by J. James)

Hilary Price remembers that her school in Much Dewchurch had 'four or five privies in a row, and a locked one for the teachers, complete with Izal paper which was smelly and hard.'

Betty Lane will never forget how the privies at school in Eye used to freeze solid in winter, and the caretaker had to light a fire to thaw them out. 'Old Jackie's boiling up the loos again!' they'd say.

Mrs J. Phillipson of Hunderton recalled that 'there were privies at Bodenham School until about 1960 – wooden seats with a hole, and a bucket underneath. Mr Dance the Headmaster could get quite cross if we asked to go to the toilet, he said toilet was something cats did, and the correct word was lavatory.' So much for education . . .

[1 0]

RANDOM REMINISCENCES

Mrs Hotchkiss lived with her in-laws while her husband was in the army during the war. 'They lived in a little cottage not far from where we live now, and they had a two-seater wooden-top toilet. When it got a bit full, my father-in-law would open up the back of the toilet and ladle the solids out into a big hole and let the liquid drain into the brook. We moved to our present cottage in 1963 and had the same sort of outside loo until 1992. My husband always emptied the old bucket every week but never grumbled. In our Golden Wedding year our landlord had a lovely bathroom and toilet put in for us in our old age. No more tin baths or loo emptying! But we honestly cannot say we have any regrets; it kept us all fit, and not so much illness either. Our old tin bath and loo are now at Acton Scott Farm Museum.'

Mollie Thomas told me that during the war an American airman and his wife were billeted at Pitfield Farm near Pembridge. Upon arrival, the American asked to use the toilet, and was directed down the garden. When he returned, he said feelingly, 'My gahd, that li'l place was sure built for speed and not for comfort!'

Some hop-pickers were lucky enough to have reasonable toilet accommodation provided for them; others had to suffer disgusting privies, or none at all, in which case they just had to find a convenient hop-vine to go behind, or a nearby field. Sometimes it was a 'tin shack' which naughty boys delighted in pelting with stones to frighten the occupants.

Miss Gwendolen Hill was born in Tudorville near Ross-on-Wye and had a strict upbringing with a rather domineering

Duncan Meakie with the remains of the shovel outside his intact two-holer at Welson.

mother. Gwendolen was forbidden to read Certain Books, so she would smuggle Edgar Wallace into the privy with her, and spend happy hours reading there. Her mother thought she must be constipated, and resorted to plying the child with a variety of purgatives, none of which seemed to have the desired effect!

Although Mrs Mary Batchelor of Saltmarshe WI was born in London, she was quite accustomed to privies when she spent her holidays with an uncle near Ross-on-Wye. In London the out-side loo had a high flush cistern and a wooden seat which stretched the width of the building. All lighting was by means of a night light or an Aladdin paraffin lamp which was placed on a small triangular corner shelf in the privy. If it was not too cold to linger, she amused herself by seeing whether she could find every letter of the alphabet on one of the squares of news-paper which hung from a nail.

In Ross, during the 20s and 30s, the privy on her uncle's farm was a long distance from the house. 'Each side of the path to it was edged with gooseberry bushes,' she told me. 'Once, when one of my cousins had partaken of too much home-made cider, he tripped and fell among the prickly gooseberries! The inside of the building, which was quite large, had a stone flagged floor, and the stone walls were whitewashed. The well-scrubbed seat had two holes, one for adults and a small one for the children. There was a long drop to the earth below and occasionally, if it was very windy, I was horrified when a piece of used paper was blown about. It was always very cold and draughty, and it was without a light. My first experience there was in 1926, and twenty years later it was still in use.'

Which brings to mind a story my husband tells about his time in India with the RAF. On a windy day a piece of used loo paper blew from the privies into the Office – he dashed in to retrieve it, but too late: the CO had signed it . . .

Mrs Hilary Price wrote to me from Wormelow. 'We have a

Long-handled scoop (or skippet) for emptying cesspits, owned by Thomas Crapper & Co Ltd. (Photo by Simon Kirby)

privy at the end of our garden,' she said, 'not in working order, and a bit overgrown, but it is a two-holer. My husband can remember using it. It's a loo with a view!

'Some older members of the family remember that when there were private matters to be discussed they would take the Tilley lamp and sit in the two-holer for hours, gossiping. My husband says when he was a child the youngsters used to creep up and try to listen to the conversations described above. "Great fun!" was his comment.

'I can recall using the outside loo at Much Dewchurch where I lived from 1942 till 1963. We used to have a wooden-seated one-holer over a tin bucket shaped like a toilet pedestal, which had to be emptied nearly every evening. We had two or three buckets to change around, and these were emptied into a hole which was dug weekly in the garden, usually under the hedge. My sister and I had to take it in turns to do this "lovely job" after Daddy died, I was eleven at the time. I hated it, and we always did it just before dark. Thank goodness we never fell in the hole.

'One neighbour had a really large pit and a metal bowl on a long stick to ladle it out over the garden every few days.

'Another job was to cut newspaper into squares, you had print on your bum sometimes, I should think! It really makes me laugh, we had lots of laughs about it all.'

Pink with embarrassment but with a twinkle in her eye, a Kington lady told me that she saw this on a privy wall in her youth:

> This is no place to sleep or slumber,
> But to fart and bolt like thunder.

Some people used to plant snowdrops alongside the garden path to light the way to the privy on the long winter evenings, and an old lady with failing eyesight used to follow a waist-high wire. I was told about one lazy man living in a row of terraced houses who sneakily used other people's privies to save himself having to empty his own bucket so often!

Sue Bowen's family privy was a two-seater some considerable distance from the house, between the greenhouse and the potting shed. Below the scrubbed seats was a cavernous pit through which the north wind whistled on a bad day. Once a year the cavern was emptied via a trapdoor in the adjoining field. 'I remember that the smell was not unpleasant,' she said, 'just a slow bacterial breaking down into something good to be dug into a trench in the garden.

'By my time there was a luxurious accommodation in the house, situated at the end of a long passage – and **that** could be tricky! Its flushing arrangements were fed from a tank in the roof, and injudicious pulling of the chain somehow upset the plumbing and someone (usually my sister who was light and a good climber) shinned up onto the roof to render first aid.

'The wooden privy up the garden was used by "kitchen folk", who went at least two at a time for company.'

Barbara Webb conjures up a delightful picture of a tiny thatched cottage in Lugwardine which she rented in the late 1950s. Its single-seater 'inconvenience' was up the garden path, a steep climb. Barbara's elderly mother and her sister came to stay, and she has 'an abiding memory of these two elegantly-dressed ladies heading up the garden path arm-in-arm and, to shield them from heavy rain, under an umbrella! **And** of course, a packet of cigarettes and a box of matches.'

Rita Lerigo told me about a family ritual that they had when she was a child. 'We had the privy at the bottom of the garden,' she said. 'It was way out in the wilds of Herefordshire, and whenever anyone had to take the long walk it was the custom to have company, so the call would go out, "Who will come to Lavender Creek with me?" The companion would then hang about, whistling and singing. But it was no joke in the wintertime.'

Margaret Wilce of Merrivale, near Ross-on-Wye, remembers that privies seemed to be always situated under trees, usually large yews. 'Grandfather always called it the Crapper, and his was at the end of a long path at the top of the garden; it was just a hole in the ground with a wooden board seat with a hole cut in the centre. It held a fascination for us grandchildren, and luckily we never suffered any ill effects despite the hot summers and flies.

'My mother, whose family has always lived in Herefordshire, usually referred to "going to the don-y-can" although we did

Mother-and-baby two-holer at Ross-on-Wye, with emptying hole at back, belonging to Mr and Mrs J. Weedon.

sometimes call it "the dyke" or "the thunderbox". Our toilet was at the side of the house under the yew trees, again a plank of wood with a hole in it; underneath was a large bucket which was purchased from the ironmonger's especially for the purpose. I had my own toilet as a child, at the side of my parents', with a much lower wooden seat and a potty underneath, which was emptied into the bucket. My father, and occasionally my mother, would empty the bucket into a hole dug in the garden; a large profusion of tomato plants grew where the bucket was emptied.'

The reference to a thunderbox reminds me of my excitement when Julia Ball told me that she lived in Thunderbox Cottage, in Pembridge! When she and her husband were house-hunting, they used to refer to it as 'the one with the thunderbox', so No 2 Westend Cottage became Thunderbox Cottage when they moved in. The house is ancient, picturesque and timber-framed, and the little oak-beamed privy appears to match it.

Under a yew tree stands the black-and-white privy behind Thunderbox Cottage in Pembridge.

This would have been a godsend to many a rural dweller, replacing the smelly bucket in the outside privy. Advertisement from the 1940s. (Reproduced by kind permission of *Home and Country*)

Sylvia Owen of Leominster wrote to me with this recollection from a time when she was about seven years old. 'We used to visit my mother's friend on a big farm. It had oil lamps all over the place. I was very afraid of the dark corners. When I needed to go, the friend took me outside, down a mucky path, and said, "There it is." She shone the lamp. To my horror, it was a wooden shed, no roof, just tin sheets to keep the rain off. It was a square piece of wood, made up with a hole, and a bucket underneath. You can imagine how I felt, as a child ... I made sure I didn't go into that place again.'

Mrs J. Phillipson of Hunderton writes: 'My family lived on Maund Bryan Common at Bodenham until 1963, when I was

A privy bucket. The large handle is for carrying when emptying the contents; the small handles are to facilitate turning the bucket into the correct position to accommodate the ladies (pointed end forward to avoid splashing; while under the seat the large handle cannot be raised to turn the bucket). Photo by Simon Kirby)

This privy bucket has been given a new lease of life with a new bottom, and découpage by owner Margaret Smith of Little Woonton Farm, near Lyonshall.

11. The primitive toilet up the garden was a tin shack, dirt floor, and a wooden seat over a pit. About 1960 our uncle put in a wooden floor, and then we had two Elsan toilets. My memories are of going up the garden in the dark with a candle, shielding the flame with my hand. My sister and I would both sit there making shadows with our hands from the candlelight, and dripping candle wax onto our nails. Father periodically cleaned out the toilet and it was all put on a dung heap in the orchard.'

Situated on the river Arrow, Eardisland is subject to serious flooding, and during the 1940s a floating privy bucket fetched up against the steps of the Cross Inn. It was half-full, and there was no doubt about what was in it . . . It was never claimed.

Janet Morgan was brought up on the Burton estate, at Grove

Farm (Eardisland) where there was a three-seater at the bottom of the garden with house leeks growing on the roof. (The ancient Greeks and Romans believed that they would protect the building from thunderbolts.) Her dad, Jim Kington, used to spend a lot of time in there, reading the *Farmers Weekly* – the family always knew where to find him when he was wanted.

Janet also remembers Rhydimoor, which had another three-seater in which the smallest hole was very low indeed, and must have been designed for very young children. Her Mum did not approve of her reading the *Beano* and the *Dandy*, but she would smuggle them into the privy and enjoy reading them there. She would often play there with her friends.

Janet's Aunt Betty used to tell her that Stretford Farm was a cider house at one time, and that to go to the loo one had to cross the yard, go under a rose arch, and right to the far end of the garden. Again the privy was a three-seater, and if one looked down the unoccupied holes the ducks could be seen swimming about on the duckpond below!

Stoke Prior WI came up with a fund of stories for me. Gill Harris told me that, as a teenager, she went to dances in Bodenham Village Hall, where there was a two-holer loo. On one occasion (which she remembers vividly) several girls came rushing back into the hall, screaming their heads off – some of the boys had put a stick down each hole, so that the girls sat down on the pointed end! Fortunately nobody was hurt, but it had given the girls a real fright. Most village halls had bucket latrines, giving rise to complaints from the neighbours about the smells; many didn't have flush toilets until the 1970s or 1980s.

Another member used to call her family's privy Rose Cottage because it was covered in roses, and situated just beyond the potato patch. Father used to empty the bucket into a trench which later got filled in. They used to call the privy 'where the

King goes alone', the direct translation of a French phrase.

A town-dweller coming to the country with her young family couldn't understand how so much of her domestic rubbish was disappearing. It turned out that her little boy was being 'helpful' by putting it down the holes in the two-seater privy.

I loved the story of 'The Shanty', which was portable. When the hole was full, Father used to move the entire privy and fill in the hole, dig another one in a different part of the garden and place the privy over it. The rhubarb was wonderful ... But I can't help imagining the kids rushing out of the house next morning, bursting to go, and yelling, 'Mum! Where's he put it *this* time?'

Barbara Morgan of Staunton-on-Arrow remembers how, when she was about six, she was taken to visit a house where there was a privy at the bottom of the garden. Having indoor plumbing at her own house, she was so enchanted with the little building that she kept asking to go to the toilet every ten minutes or so, all afternoon.

Topsy Price of Upton Bishop recalls that when she joined the Women's Land Army in 1939, her first shock after leaving her modern home was the walk up the garden to the privy at her digs. In the early 40s she went looking for a distant relative who lived in the area. Another shock! Here, too, the privy was 'up the long path, up steps to a long wooden seat with one large and one small hole ... squares of newspaper on a string hung on a nail, and only half a door, with a shovel to take around the back where there was a pile of ashes from the fire to cover over one's efforts.

'Another cottage where I had digs was one of three, and the loo there was halfway up a long garden. It was a large, square stone building with a heavy door and no light, and always seemed damp. There was a wooden seat with a wooden cover, and a handle to lift it. There was a huge cavity below, which

84

A family of five used this two-holer at Birley until 1976. (Photo by Bill Probert)

must have run along the back of the three cottages. The cold draught coming up when the lid was lifted was enough to freeze anyone's nether regions.'

Bill Probert of Birley has a privy in his garden which he remembers using as a child. He says, 'It's a double dwelling, there was two side by side, one large and one small, it was a two seater. It was a pit, and Father used to put lime in to dispose of anything in the pit. We were five in the family and we all had to use it. About 1940 I moved it to the other side of the garden to make it more private. I put a concrete base down and then used the bucket.

'I can well remember digging a path to it when the snow was here, and had to dig again next morning because more snow had fell and covered the path. Father or me had to dispose of the contents in the garden when no one was about, mostly at night. We used it up till about 1976 when the owner of the house had a bathroom and toilet put inside the house, but the old toilet is still standing in the same place, as a garden shed now, and a home for the grey squirrel. So the old Privy has had a long life like me – I'm over 80.'

A fellow-imbiber at the Compasses Inn in Wigmore told me this one: Auntie had come to stay; it was a long journey from Town, and when she arrived she was desperate to go. 'Where is it?' she asked as soon as she arrived. They told her. She wasn't used to privies, like, but off she went like greased lightning, and shot into the privy. She sat straight down with a thump, not realising that there was a lid with a knob-handle in the middle, over the hole. It must have been painful, it went right up her bum! Anyhow, she yelled like anything, and pissed all over the place.

Priscilla Davies remembers Greenhill Farm at Wigmore, where there was a two-holer earth-house, or closet, with a small hayloft above it called a tollet; from this there was a door to the pig-run. She and her sisters used to venture out carrying a candle in a jamjar by its string handle, ostensibly to do either 'light jobs' or 'heavy jobs'. It was a two-holer, and the girls would lower the jamjar into one of the holes, watching in fascination as the rats became mesmerised by the light, frozen into rodent statues, their eyes gleaming in the darkness.

There was an ash path to the earth-house. The pit was limed, and half the waste dug out yearly, the other half the following year; it was spread on the marrow bed, which resulted in superb marrows, and the liquid waste soaked into the brook. After the weekly wash, the soapy water was used to scrub the spotless privy seats, and emptied down the holes.

Thomas had spent the whole day cleaning out the gubban-hole. 'T'ent a very clean job, mind,' he said. 'When I started, ur smelt smartish; but when I'd done, by God, ur stank roarin'!' The house at poo corner?

A young couple had just moved into their new modern home, and invited the old folks in for a meal. Father went to use the loo and was away so long that his wife said, 'You'd better go and see if he's all right, son.' He came back shouting, 'Come quick, Dad has gone blue and I think he's dead!' The woman went to look and said, 'Silly old devil, he's holding his breath waiting to hear the splat.' They had a privy at home where it took a long time for the stuff to hit bottom, and the man always counted, holding his breath at the same time, to see how long it took.

This tale was told to me by Johnny Williams of Pembridge – I'd heard it before, but it *could* be true! A visitor complained that there was no lock on the privy door. 'What would 'er want a lock for?' said the owner. 'No one ever pinched a bucket from thur yet.'

[11]

PULLING THE PLUG ON PRIVIES

The village in which I live is one which does not yet have mains drainage, and Mayglothling's Waste Disposal tankers in action are a common sight. My house is one of a row of Tudor-style dwellings built by Border Oak, the local specialist firm which uses similar building techniques to those by which genuine Tudor houses were raised. Set in the centre of the communal lawn in front of our houses is a 'Tudor dovecote', which attracts the attention of passing tourists who photograph it excitedly, never dreaming that the pretty little building contains a septic tank!

I discovered that ours is unique; others like it conceal oil tanks for central heating, but ours is the only one that hides sewage arrangements. An article in *The Birmingham Post* described it as 'the prettiest septic tank in the West Midlands'. Now I feel really proud of it!

Even today, sanitary arrangements are occasionally somewhat primitive, notably at open-air county events – often a simple tent containing a chemical toilet where loud singing or coughing is recommended to indicate its occupancy ... Mobile loos go one better, providing decently-equipped cubicles and washbasins with running water, but they cost more to hire.

Toilets on trains have changed little since the first was introduced, with the excrement dropping directly onto the tracks; hence the rule 'do not use while train is standing in station' still holds good.

Many people and firms such as Elemental Solutions of Orcop are returning to the concept of indoor earth closets, as they can

Today's waste disposal tanker, dealing with the septic tank uniquely concealed by a 20th century 'Tudor dovecote' in Eardisland.

be both hygienic and environmentally sound – no smell, no splash. They also advocate recycling 'greywater' (bath and washing-up water), as wasting water is now a major problem.

Did you know that 29 waterless urinals were installed in the Millennium Dome?

Nowadays we sit in the warmth and comfort of our homes to do our business – but how times change! Sex is explicit on TV, but not defecation. In spite of the modern anything-goes attitude to life, most people today would be shocked at the thought of sharing their private performances with other people, even close family members. And yet, only a few decades ago, it was still considered perfectly normal to share a multiholer privy with family and friends.

Tomorrow's loo? Rosie and Adam Adamson of Broad Oak admire the DOWMUS, an *indoor* compost loo, recommended by Elemental Solutions of Orcop. This state of the art, waterless modern 'privy' is developed in Herefordshire, in partnership with the Australian designer. No smell, no splash! (Photo by Nick Grant)

The bad old days, or the good old days? A little of each, perhaps, but for the most part fondly remembered.

> A Hereford fellow named Hyde
> Fell into a privy and died.
> His unfortunate brother
> Fell into another
> And now they're interred side by side.

AND FINALLY ... I do hope that all privy owners who read this book will continue to take a pride in that little garden house, and realise what a treasure they possess – an antique, not valuable in cash terms perhaps, but a priceless part of our Herefordian heritage, well worth preserving for posterity.

A PRIVY BY ANY OTHER NAME

Bog
Boghouse
Closet
Convenience
Crapper
Crap-house
Don-y-can
Dub
Duff
Dungy
Dunny
Dyke
Earth closet
Earth house
Garden house
Garden loo
Garderobe
Geudy (Welsh, pronounced
  'goo-I-dy')
Going:
  behind a bush
  down the garden
  for a Jimmy Riddle
  for a shit
  for a slash
  for a Tom Tit
  to do woopsies
  to feed the chickens
  to feed the pigs

to inspect the plumbing
to pay a visit
to pick daisies
to pluck a rose
to point my weapon at the
  target
to point Percy at the
  porcelain
to powder my nose
to see a man about a dog
to see which way the
  wind's blowing
to shake the dew off the lily
to shut up the hens
to spend a penny
to wash my hands
to water the flowers
to wring my socks out
up Lavender Creek
up the garden
where the King goes alone
Gong house
Gubban-hole
Heads
Here 'tis
Holy of Holies
House of Commons
Houses of Par-li-a-ment
Inconvenience

Ivy Cottage
Jakes
Karzi
Latrine
Lav
Lavvy
Lavatory
Lem Putt
Little boys' room
Little girls' room
Little house
Loo
Necessarium
Necessary house
Out the back
Penny house
Place of easement
Reading room
Reredorter
Rose Cottage
Shanty
Shit-hole
Shit-house

Smallest room
The house at poo corner
The house where the
    Emperor goes on foot
The jakes
The John
The long drop
The opportunities
The ping-pong-po
The proverbial
The tandem (two-holer)
The throne-room
The wee house
The wot-yer-callit
Thunderbox
Ty bach (Welsh: 'little
    house', pronounced 'tee-
    bah')
Urinal
Used beer department
Waterloo
Widdlehouse
'Yer Tiz'

ACKNOWLEDGEMENTS

Firstly, my thanks to Countryside Books who helped me to fulfil a life-long ambition to actually write a book. I've been approaching publishers for over fifty years – with varying degrees of success – but this is the first time that anyone has approached *me*!

One or two people were a bit po-faced (pun intended) when I contacted them, and thought that I 'could have found something nicer to write about', and a few didn't answer my letters; but they were the exception – everyone else was very, very helpful.

Many busy firms have taken the time and trouble to help me – notably Archaeological Investigations Ltd (Dr John C. Eisel), Armitage Shanks (Sam Woodberry), the Avoncroft Museum of Historic Buildings near Bromsgrove (Dr Simon Penn), BBC Hereford & Worcester, Caradon Plumbing Solutions (Terry Woolliscroft), the County Record Office (Sue Hubbard), Thomas Crapper & Co Ltd (Simon Kirby), Elemental Solutions (Nick Grant), the Gladstone Working Pottery Museum (Angela Lee), the Herefordshire Council (Paul Gibbons, Conservation Architect), the *Hereford Journal*, the *Hereford Times*, the Hereford Waterworks Museum (Dr Noel Meeke), Leominster Museum staff, Mayglothling Waste Services of Kington, the *Mid Wales Journal* and the *Ross Gazette*.

I would also like to thank the owners/managers/agents of castles and stately homes such as Eastnor Castle, the Garnons estate, Kentchurch Court, Wigmore Abbey and Wilton Castle for their courtesy in allowing me to invade their privacy. TV antiques expert Henry Sandon also deserves special mention for his kindness.

WI members and friends all over the county have been a tremendous help, putting up posters for me, getting my requests for help into their parish magazines and, of course, sending me photographs and telling me of their experiences with privies.

My sincere apologies to all those who took the trouble to write or phone, to send me photos, or spared the time to clear out their garden sheds to reveal their sanitary origins for me to photograph, and whose stories and pictures have been omitted from this book. In the end I was so overwhelmed with material that I had the painful task of eliminating nearly half.

I've had a wonderful time researching our Herefordshire privies – I've been to so many lovely places, and met so many interesting people. To everyone who has helped in any way in the compiling of this book, and particularly to my long-suffering husband Peter, I offer my most grateful thanks.